Alexis,
Follo your dreams

THE
ADVENTURES
OF THE
SOUL SISTAS

(or How the Sisters
Changed the World)

Written by
NEWTON VANRIEL

Illustrated by
MONIQUE RA BRENT

◆ FriesenPress

One Printers Way
Altona, MB R0G 0B0
Canada

www.friesenpress.com

ISBN
978-1-03-912331-1 (Hardcover)
978-1-03-912330-4 (Paperback)
978-1-03-912332-8 (eBook)

1. FAMILY & RELATIONSHIPS, ADOPTION & FOSTERING

Distributed to the trade by The Ingram Book Company

This book is dedicated to my mother and my wife—
our true superheroes!

"There is nothing better than love."
Luther Vandross

THE BEGINNING!

It was a sunny day in Toronto. The warm glow of June.

At the market, Alexandra was excited. It was her first day hosting a booth to sell her custom-made jewellery. She had graduated from graphic design school and was ready to take on the world!

Out of the corner of her eye, she spots a man—a lovely man—looking at her.

He seemed familiar, and then she realized she had met him at a graphic design social a few months ago. It wasn't hard to miss him. He was the only Black person at that conference network session of more than one thousand people.

Alexandra didn't realize he was staring at her. She thought to herself, *Great smile and his artwork is amazing.*

Nathan recognized her too. He was impressed by how she spoke about what she enjoys and her really cool leather jacket.

He walked over to her stand and started talking to her. They talked about how they both loved the same books and art. Six hours passed by quickly.

She had ignored everyone who stopped by; Nathan was so interesting, though his jokes were corny.

Nathan Spirit was a pastor's son who had left Jamaica at age five. He grew up in public housing and walked with a strut and a sense of purpose. He had big dreams.

Alexandra Rochelle was a daughter of a doctor and professor who left Trinidad at age two. You would never know her family status, though—she drove an old, beat-up car and loved army surplus stores. She had big dreams, too! She wanted to do something good in this big world.

Nathan bravely decided to become her instant assistant and stood in the stand next to her all day.

Maybe he's crazy, Alexandra thought, *but let's go with the flow.*

What began as a lovely day in the sunshine was the start of an inseparable bond.

MOVING!

Who knew falling in love would be that easy? Two years later, Nathan and Alexandra got married on another sunny day.

These independent souls moved into a one-bedroom apartment and loved their day-to-day life. Both worked online in their graphic design business; it would be easy to move and begin their adventure!

Alexandra was not into talking about her family's wealth. She would modestly say that her family was doing okay.

Her father owned a large farm in Espanola, a town in northern Ontario where Nathan had never been.

Her dad's business partner put money into fifty-acres of cornfields and chicken coops. Truly country.

One day, suddenly, her father died of a heart attack.

Time passed. After a while, Alexandra's mother told her that she and Nathan were now proud owners of a fifty-acre farm.

What would two city people do in the country?

After much soul-searching, they decided to do it. They were country now!

THE JOURNEY

The sounds of the daylight
Brighten up the skies.
No more beautiful than the twinkle in your eyes.
A new beginning—oh, so bright.
Sunny days on the farm,
Ohhh, what a delight!

THE FARM!

Nathan and Alexandra loved their farm in the polite town of Espanola (polite, but no one invited them to any pool parties or town fairs), but they enjoyed life on the farm while working on their successful online business.

Though each day brought them happiness, they felt like something was missing . . . a baby to bring more joy to their lives.

LET'S HAVE A BABY!

They had tried to have a baby.

They asked, "Why can't we have a child?" It was very important to them.

They even built a huge library with books of all types. But, no baby.

They were surrounded by so much happiness but felt a sense of sadness, too.

The beautiful dream created stress, but they always found hope.

Each Saturday in the summer, Espanola held a small farmers' market. Alexandra and Nathan continued their tradition and had a stall for Alexandra's jewellery business.

One day, a pregnant young Irish woman with flaming red hair, was interested in some classic design earrings. Her name was Yvonne. She was about twenty years old, and they had an instant connection. Yvonne shared her love for unique jewelry, and Alexandra couldn't stop asking Yvonne about her growing belly.

Alexandra even invited her over for dinner a few times.

Yvonne was moving to Florida in less than a year for a new job opportunity! She was eight months pregnant and was thinking about giving up her child for adoption. It was a tough decision.

Yvonne had already spoken to the adoption agency, who started the paperwork.

Over time, they'd gotten to know each other, and Yvonne realized Alexandra and Nathan would make amazing parents. They both wondered about adopting a white child who looked different—but love is love! It didn't matter.

The local adoption official also lived in Espanola. She was initially concerned about the quick pace of the request—polite and hesitant about two Black parents adopting a white child—but she knew the Spirit family and helped them process the request.

Then their waiting and praying began. *It should happen soon*, they thought, *right?*

It happened! After months of waiting and hoping, the Sprit family was approved!

CHARM!

Their process was approved! Sunshine was restored to the Spirit family!

They had adopted a baby girl, and Charm was to be her name.

Yvonne then moved to Florida, secure that she had made the right decision.

CHARM

A gift is here,
A wonder to see.
It is so clear. She brings a renewed glee.
The puzzle of life is closer to full form.
Now we are happy, a calm in the storm.

When it rains, it pours—in a good way.

The Spirit family wanted to have another sibling for Charm. The opportunity and meeting happened at the market again!

A young Black woman named Vivienne hosted a kiosk serving Jamaican patties. She was new to the area and had gotten a great scholarship to Oxford. Vivienne was seven months pregnant and about to become a single parent.

She, too, had registered to put the baby up for adoption and wasn't sure if it was fair for the Spirit family to have another newborn.

12

The Spirits wondered, *Is this too much for us?* They had a stable household, a big farm, and had already gone through the challenges of the first adoption. They prayed and knew it was the right decision. Their paperwork was processed, more prayers were made, and then they received a call.

They could adopt another newborn! More sunny days; Dawn was here!

DAWN!

DAWN

A new day is dawning, and we are feeling good.
Our family is complete, like we knew it would.
With more sunshine and laughter,
We are blessed in every way.
Let's celebrate the dawn and greet each new day!

FARM ADVENTURES⊠ TALK OF THE TOWN!

The Soul Sistas, as they nicknamed the girls, were only born eight months apart! Indeed, what a unique family, filled with lots of love. Could we be any happier?

HAPPINESS ON THE FARM

With Charm and Dawn,
What treasures they will find,
Soul Sistas in their own mind.
People may look—what is this?
The sisters don't care.
They live in bliss,
With nothing to fear!

15

The young girls were the talk of the town. No one had ever seen a family like this. "So different," they would say. A family of two Black parents and two girls. One baby with dark skin and a full afro. The other was a red-haired, fair-skinned baby with freckles.

The townspeople weren't rude; they just smiled in a civil manner—in a Canadian way.

Though it seemed the town was warming to the couple, cars would slowly pass their kiosk, which was strange.

People would line up at the farmers' market at a distance to watch and look at the girls. In the beginning, it was okay. But every day? Not so much.

The girls were bright, entertaining, and LOUD! They didn't care that people looked. They were just happy to be sisters.

JUST LIKE TWINS!

In the beginning, the Spirits realized one thing. Both Charm and Dawn would cry when they were separated. Such loud cries that you could hear them a mile away!

One time Dawn had to go to the doctor because Alexandra and Nathan thought she had chickenpox.

She did!

So, Charm grabbed a marker and drew dots all over her face. They could still be twins!

Charm's first words were, "I'm Dawn."

Dawn's first word was, "Charm."

They wanted to wear the same clothes all the time; same clothes and same colours—the same everything!

They would stand in front of each other and smile, copying each other as babies in every way.

The Spirits jokingly started calling them twins, but the townspeople didn't understand it. They smiled and kept their distance.

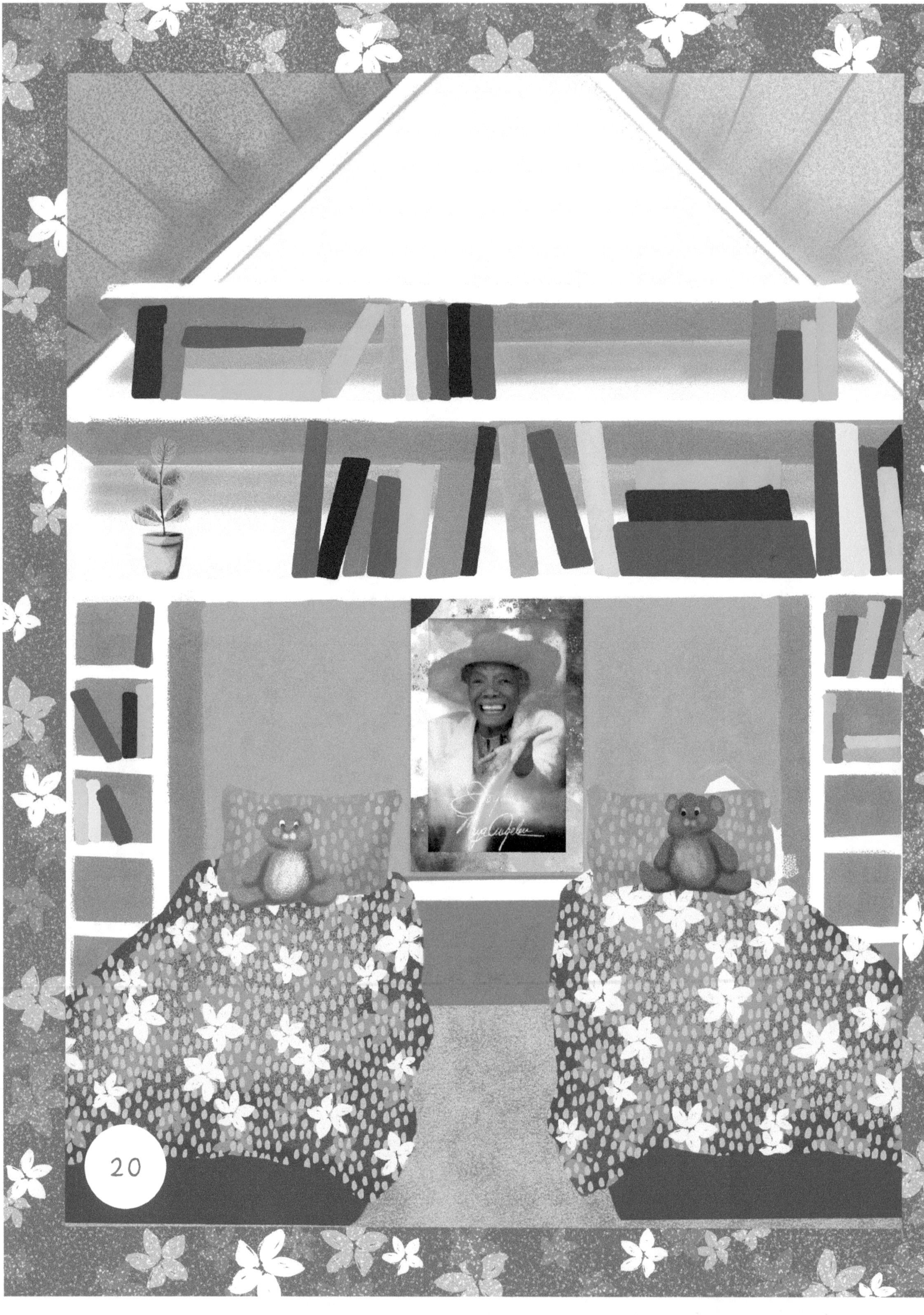

THE WORLD OF BOOKS!

Charm and Dawn's major bond was over books.

Even before they could understand the words, Nathan, an avid reader, had all types of books in his huge library, though few were children's books. Charm and Dawn would listen as each parent took turns reading a bedtime story from authors like James Baldwin, Malcolm Gladwell, D. H. Lawrence, Shakespeare, and books such as the Bible.

Before they were potty-trained, the girls would repeat quotes and verses from their parents. Alexandra and Nathan realized how smart the Soul Sistas were. *Too smart for their own good*, they thought. But it was a good thing.

Even when Charm and Dawn couldn't read, they would nibble on the books, much to the annoyance of Nathan, who was more structured and believed in following formal education courses. While Alexandra wanted the girls to express their individualities. But don't eat the books.

Many of the books the Spirits were looking for weren't available in local libraries and schools.

They wanted more diversity and more worldly views. The girls wanted nothing to do with playing with "baby" toys and no video games for them.

Charm and Dawn were determined to be the same in everything they did, and their parents thought it was unique. Their more traditional family members muttered, "Weird," under their breaths. The townspeople just smiled and kept a distance, politely.

One day, Alexandra and Nathan tried to place the girls in separate beds, but the girls would hop into each other's beds every night.

OUR FRIENDS!

The farm was the girls' playground, and many areas on the property were their playpen. The chickens became their friends. Both parents loved jerk chicken, but they never mentioned eating it in front of the girls!

CHICKENS ARE THE BEST!

My chickens can talk.
Don't believe what they say,
Chickens are the smartest in every way.
My chicken can read a book,
I even saw Doris, the chicken, cook.
You should never eat chicken stew,
It may be your friend in all that goo.

23

OUR FARM SCHOOL

The sisters even spoke their own language, flipping words backwards. Bird became Drib. They loved how they understood each other!

At the age of four, they could read books. They read to each other in their farm school, and they held a "darg" and handed out papers to all their toys, who were also their friends.

THE WEIRD FAMILY?

Their own family thought of them as unique, but the community was hesitant to embrace this strange mix.

They even heard people say, "How can a Black family raise a white child?" Alexandra and Nathan's extended family thought they should move back to Toronto for an easier life, but the Spirits were home with their family on the farm.

The sisters thought that they were just fine!

WEIRD?

What's weird to you may be what you see.
The beauty within may make some flee.
Don't be afraid, and you may find,
The beauty within and the power of the positive mind.
So—be weird!

28

SOUL SISTAS' WORLD

The Spirit girls were never invited to local children's parties. They were okay with it because they enjoyed their own Supa Sistas' World right there on the farm.

Their toys became characters in the big world fantasy of the Supa Sistas.

The stuffed bear became the big-school principal, who took away people's fun.

The other stuffed toys became the other kids.

The Supa Sistas were here to save the world from "no sharing people" who took away people's games, fun, and joy.

SCHOOL BEGINS!

It was time for Charm and Dawn to begin school. They cried. They didn't want to go into the big world; they wanted to stay home.

The other kids could not understand their reverse-word language, and the girls were way ahead in reading and math skills of the kindergarten kids. Would they be bored?

Many of the townspeople had already made fun of how they always wore the same clothes. And they had already said, "You can't have the same mommy."

Both girls promised that they would be Soul Sistas forever. The farm, with their animal friends, had become their world. Now it was time for Charm and Dawn to enter the "Big World."

CPSIA information can be obtained
at www.ICGtesting.com
Printed in the USA
BVHW021038181122
R14285300002B/R142853PG651948BVX00033B/1

9 781039 123304